Catwise

I wish to proclaim
that I love life
to distraction.

ALBERT CAMUS

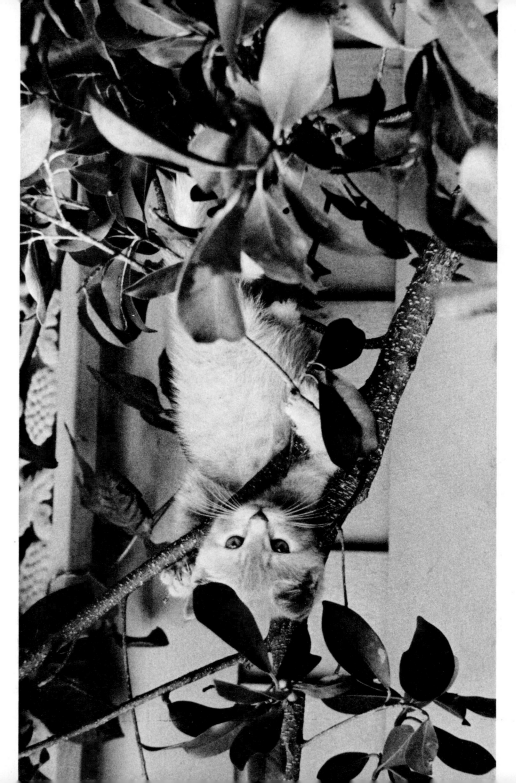

Catwise

WILBUR PIPPIN ✳ MARIAN WINTERS

Hutchinson

Hutchinson & Co (Publishers) Ltd
3 Fitzroy Square, London W1P 6JD

Hutchinson Group (Australia) Pty Ltd
30-32 Cremorne Street, Richmond South, Victoria 3121, Australia

London, Melbourne, Sydney, Auckland,
Wellington, Johannesburg, and agencies
throughout the world

First published 1979

© 1979 by Wilbur Pippin and Marian Winters

Published by arrangement with Alfred A. Knopf Inc.

Printed and bound in the United States of America

ISBN 0 09 140281 6

The authors wish to thank the following people for their assistance in producing Catwise:

The great writers, poets and philosophers who have stimulated man's mind and uplifted his spirit through the centuries, and Nancy Nicholas, who has provided invaluable guidance and encouragement in the present.

Richard Chipley, who gave of his time and his graphic sense.

Tom Wier, who helped birth, raise and cherish all thirty-six subjects.

The Burton Tuckers, who care for them.

Catwise

I never wonder to see men wicked,
but I often wonder not to see them ashamed.

It is a
world to see!

JOHN LYLY

The greatest prayer
is patience.

BUDDHA

There is little friendship in the world.

FRANCIS BACON

Adventurers
accomplish
great things.

MONTESQUIEU

What a time,
what a civilization!

MARCUS CICERO

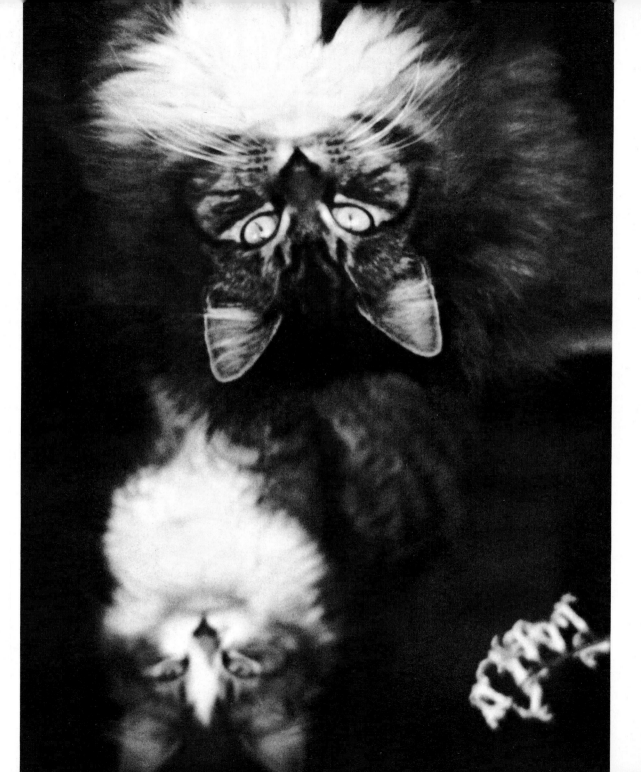

It is our
own vanity
that makes
the vanity
of others
intolerable
to us.

LA ROCHEFOUCAULD

In that
sweet mood
when
pleasant
thoughts
bring
sad
thoughts
to the mind.

WILLIAM WORDSWORTH

The rapture
of pursuing
is the prize.

HENRY WADSWORTH LONGFELLOW

*If eyes
were made
for seeing,
then
beauty
is its own
excuse
for being.*

RALPH WALDO EMERSON

Dignity consists not in possessing honors, but in the consciousness that we deserve them.

ARISTOTLE

My way of joking
is to tell the truth.
It's the funniest joke
in the world.

GEORGE BERNARD SHAW

*Fortune is not
on the side of
the faint-hearted.*

SOPHOCLES

He that can have patience, can have what he will.

BENJAMIN FRANKLIN

A laugh
is worth
a hundred groans
in any market.

CHARLES LAMB

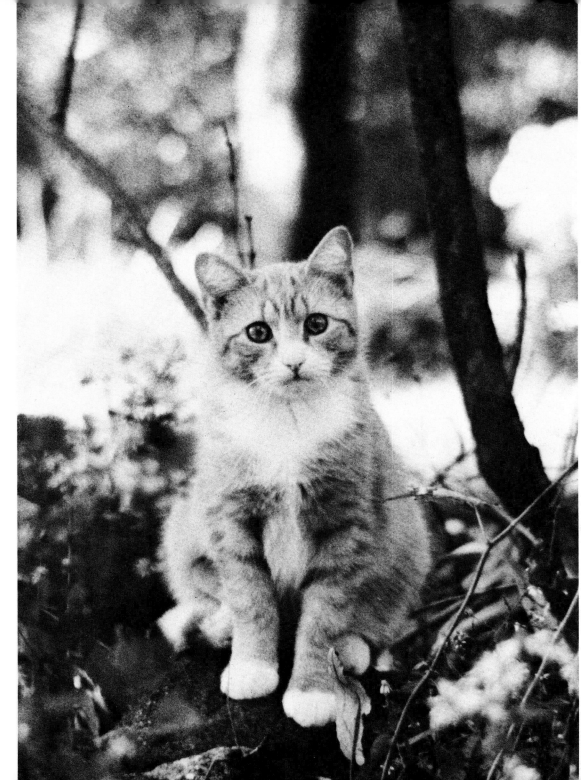

Adolescence
is certainly far
from
a uniformly
pleasant
period.

DON MARQUIS

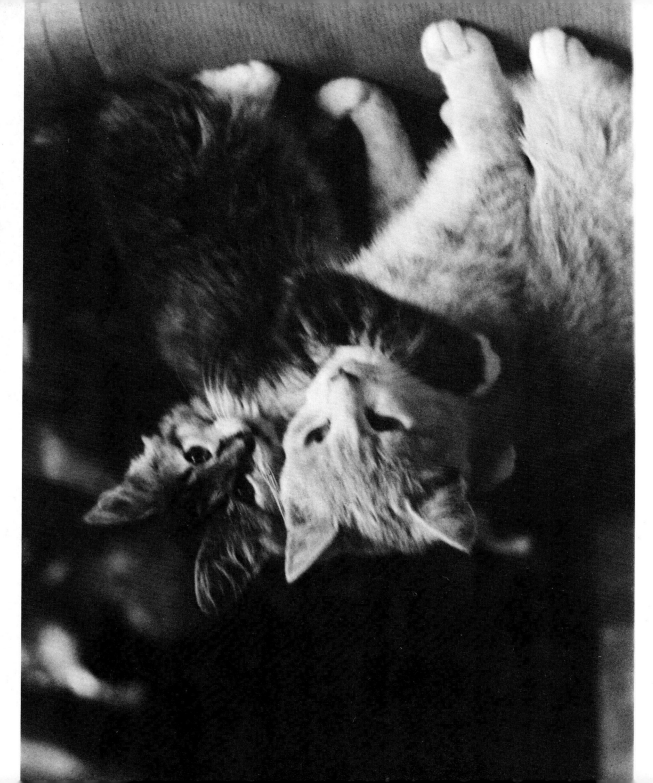

What a
melancholy world
this would be
without children.

SAMUEL TAYLOR COLERIDGE

Suspicion is the poison
of true friendship.

SAINT AUGUSTINE

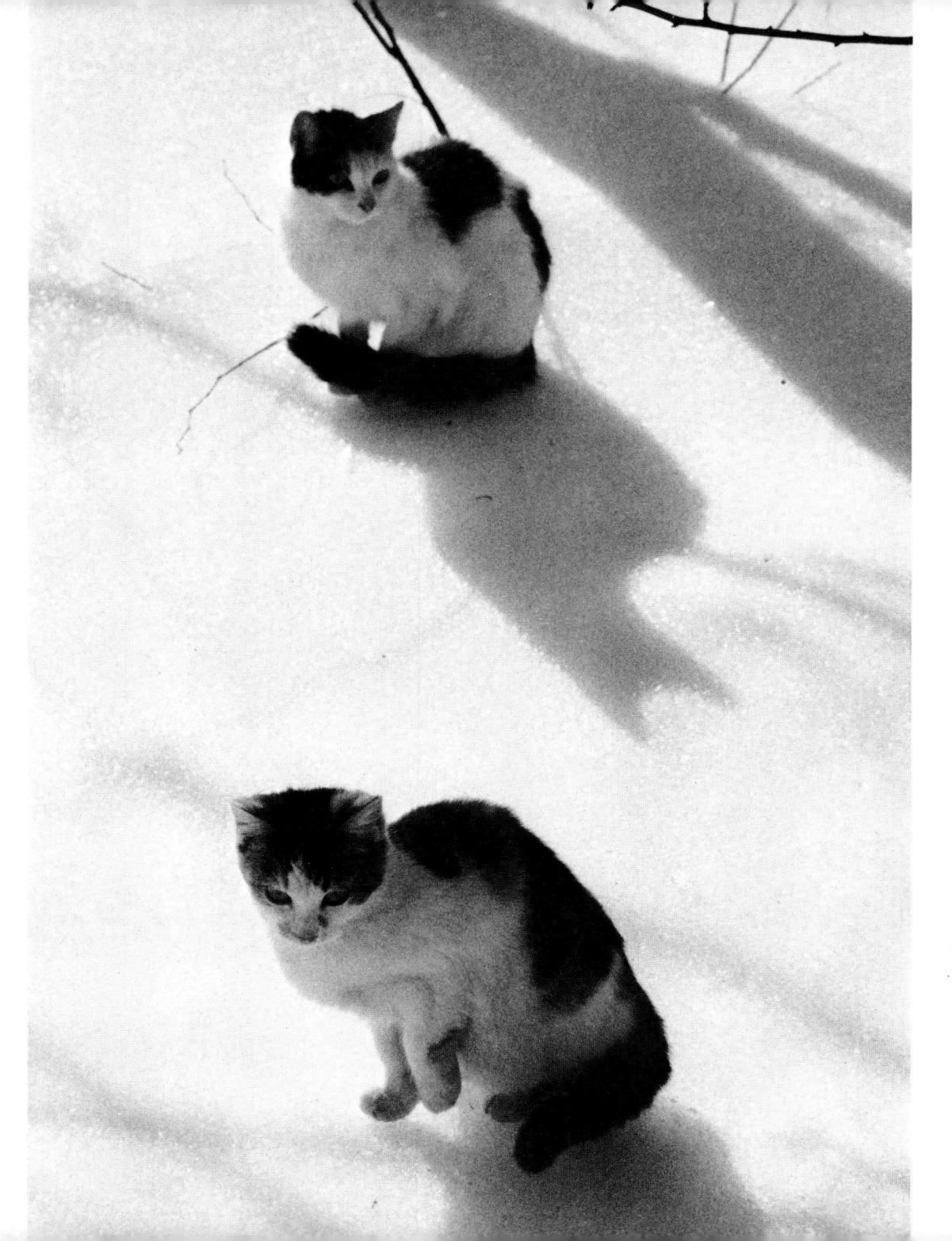

*Patience is
so like fortitude
that she seems
either her sister
or her daughter.*

ARISTOTLE

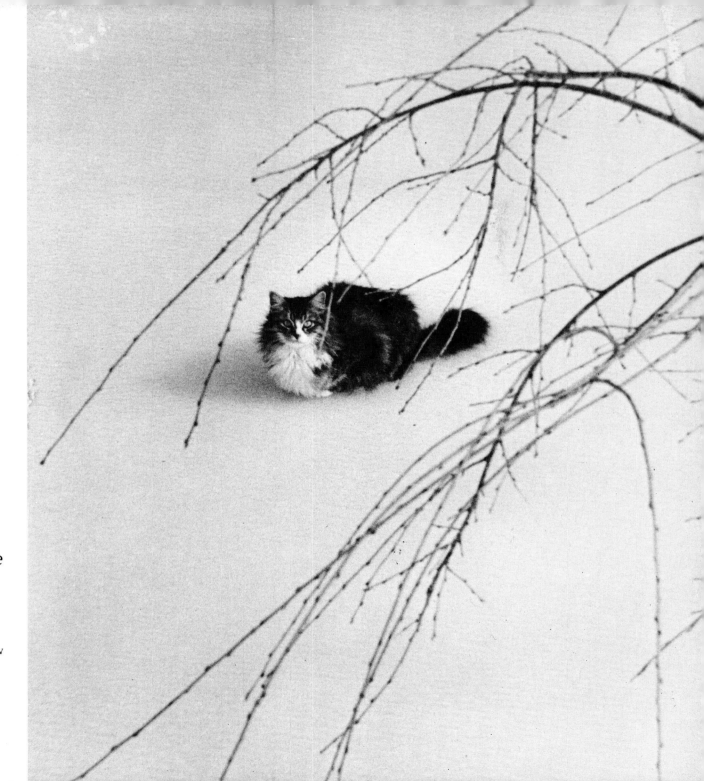

What a strange power there is in silence!

RALPH WALDO EMERSON

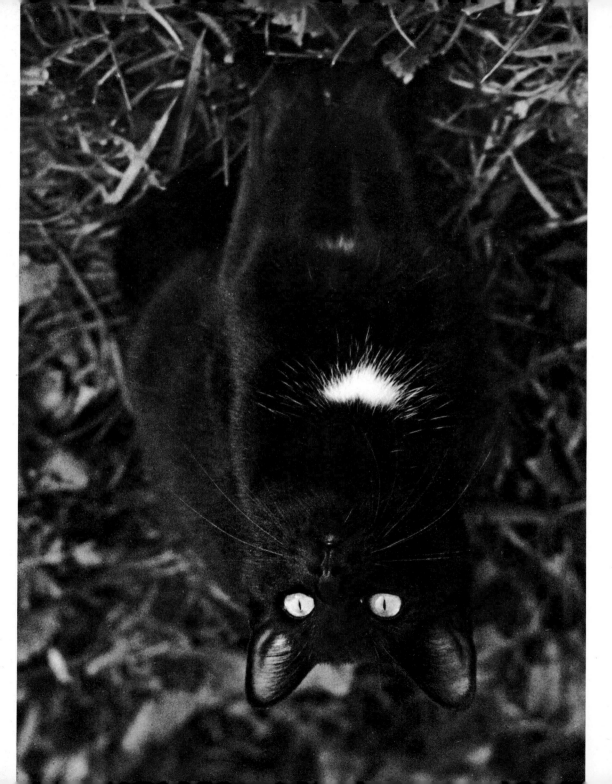

Enthusiasm,
nothing great
was ever achieved
without it.

RALPH WALDO EMERSON

Have you known
how to take repose?
You have done more
than he who has
taken cities
and empires.

MONTAIGNE

The greatest remedy for anger is delay.

SENECA

*Steep yourself
in a bowl
of summertime.*

VIRGIL

*Bashfulness
may sometimes
exclude
pleasure.*

SAMUEL JOHNSON

The world is full
of poetry,
the air is living
with its spirit.

JAMES GATES PERCIVAL

To be suspicious is to invite treachery.

VOLTAIRE

*Who never climbs
as rarely falls.*

JOHN GEEENLEAF WHITTIER

*Thy modesty's
a candle
to thy merit.*

HENRY FIELDING

I really only have perfect fun with myself.

Pity is best taught by fellowship in woe.

SAMUEL TAYLOR COLERIDGE

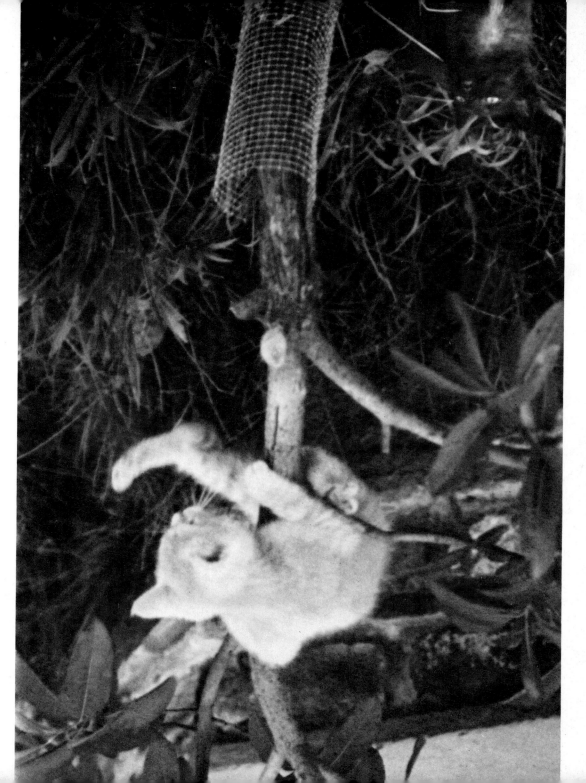

Fields have eyes
and woods have ears.

THOMAS HEYWOOD

Mortifications
are often
more painful than
real calamities.

OLIVER GOLDSMITH

A pessimist is a man who thinks everybody as nasty as himself and hates them for it.

GEORGE BERNARD SHAW

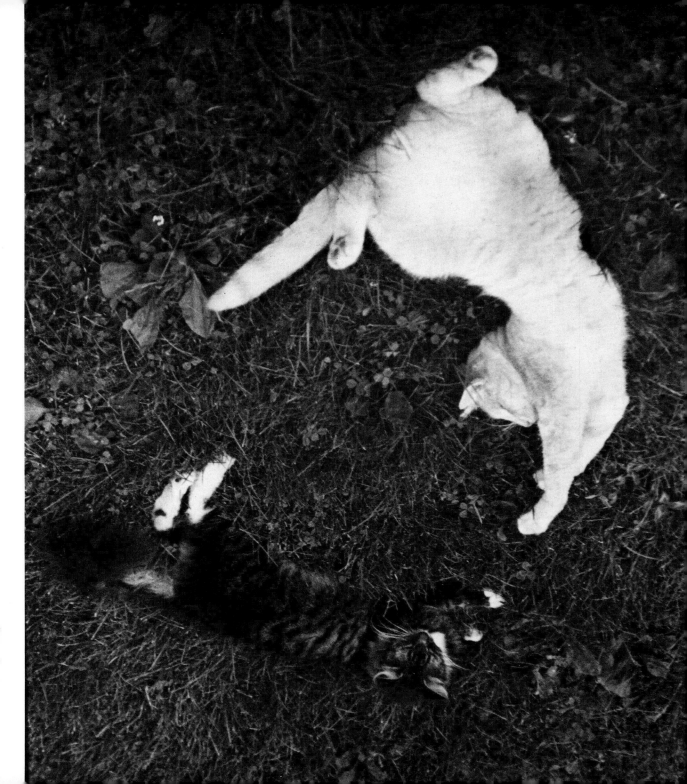

If she undervalues me,
what care I
how fair she be?

SIR WALTER RALEIGH

Society is no comfort to one not sociable.

WILLIAM SHAKESPEARE

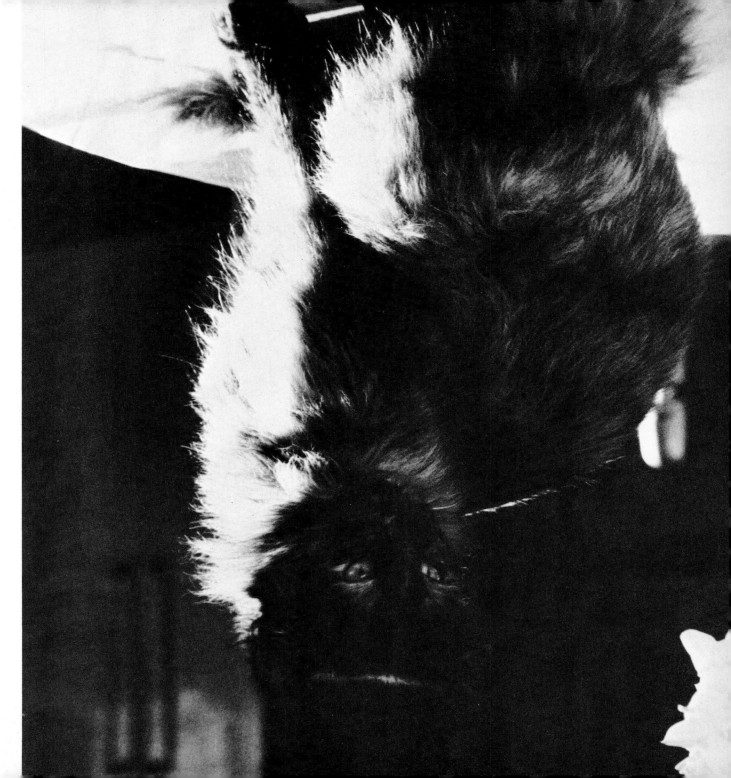

Beauty is not so much
a quality of the object
beheld, as an effect
in him who beholds it.

BENEDICT SPINOZA

*Nature is company
enough for me.*

WILLIAM HAZLITT

Avoid
popularity.
It has many
snares and
no real
benefit.

WILLIAM PENN

If you would sleep soundly, take a clear conscience to bed with you.

BENJAMIN FRANKLIN

They can conquer who believe they can.

VIRGIL

Who can explain
the secret pathos
of nature's
loveliness?

HENRY VAN DYKE

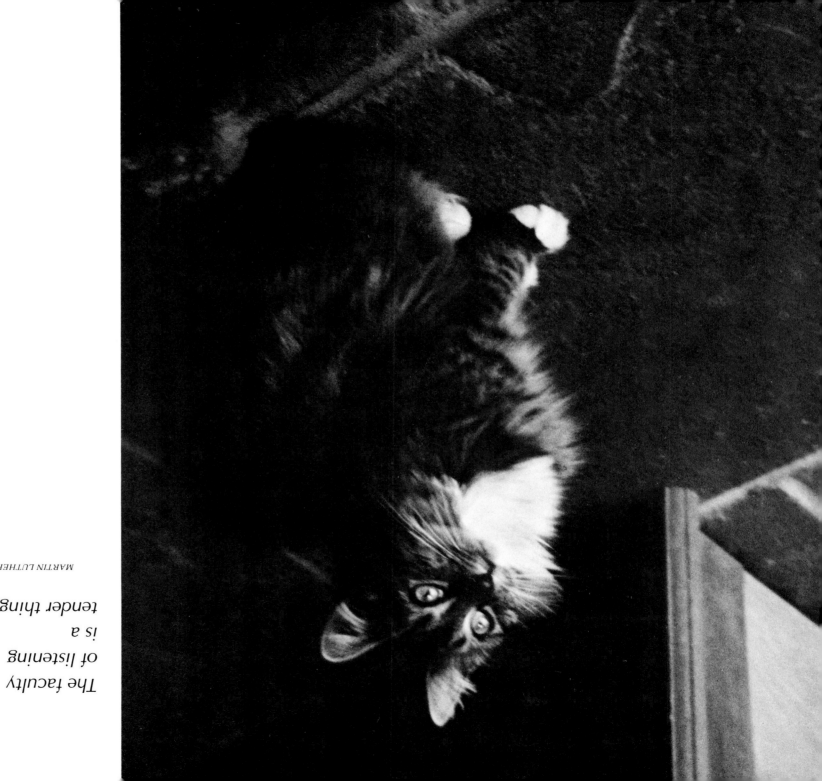

The faculty
of listening
is a
tender thing.

MARTIN LUTHER

Life is not a spectacle or a feast; it is a predicament.

GEORGE SANTAYANA

*Nature I'll court
in her
sequestered
haunts.*

TOBIAS SMOLLETT

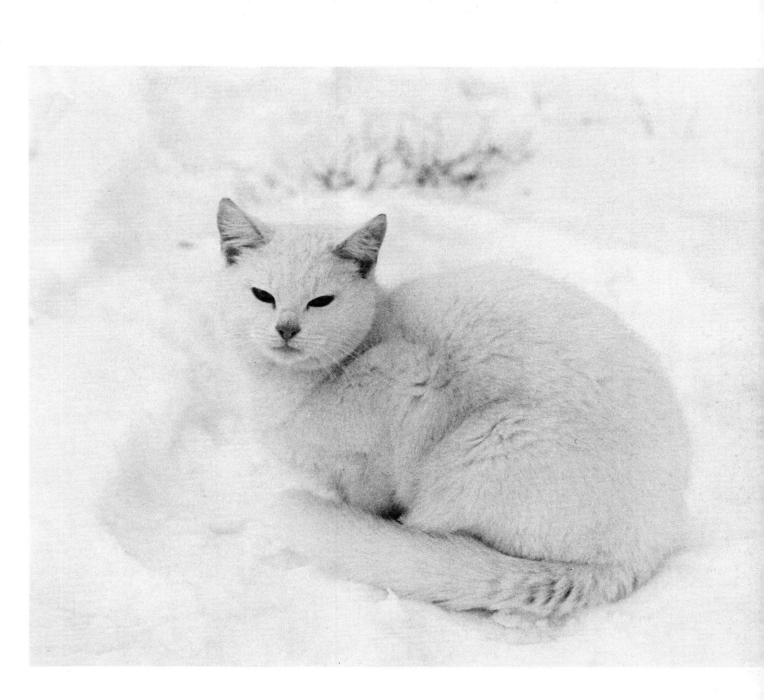

The silence
of the place
was like a sleep;
so full of rest
it seemed.

HENRY WADSWORTH LONGFELLOW

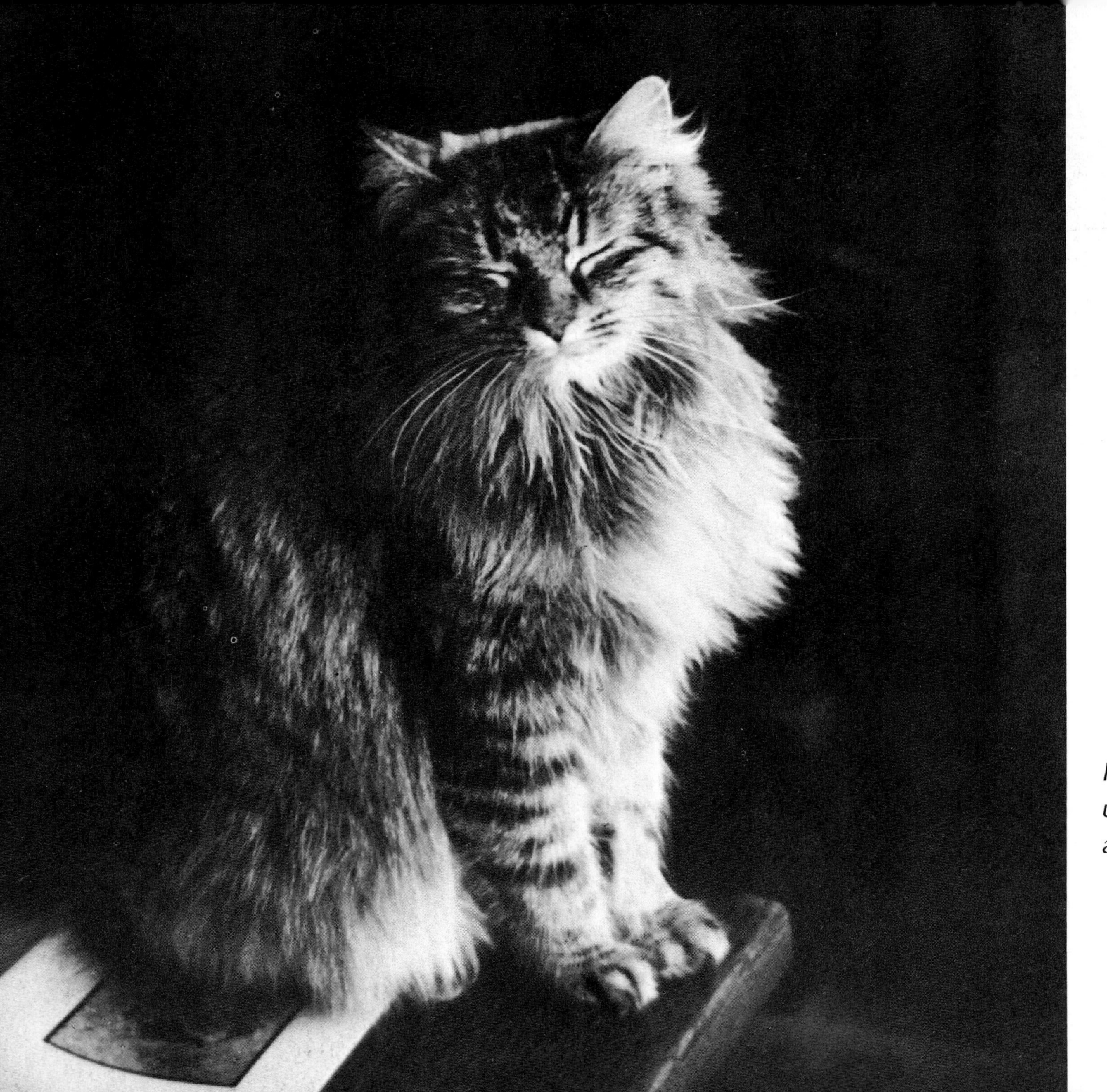

*I could reflect
upon many pleasing
adventures I have had.*

*Unnumbered spirits
round thee fly.*

ALEXANDER POPE

*I would choose
to make a bargain
with a good decent
family who have every day
a tolerable dinner.*

JAMES BOSWELL

*The slander of some
is as great a
recommendation as
the praise
of others.*

HENRY FIELDING

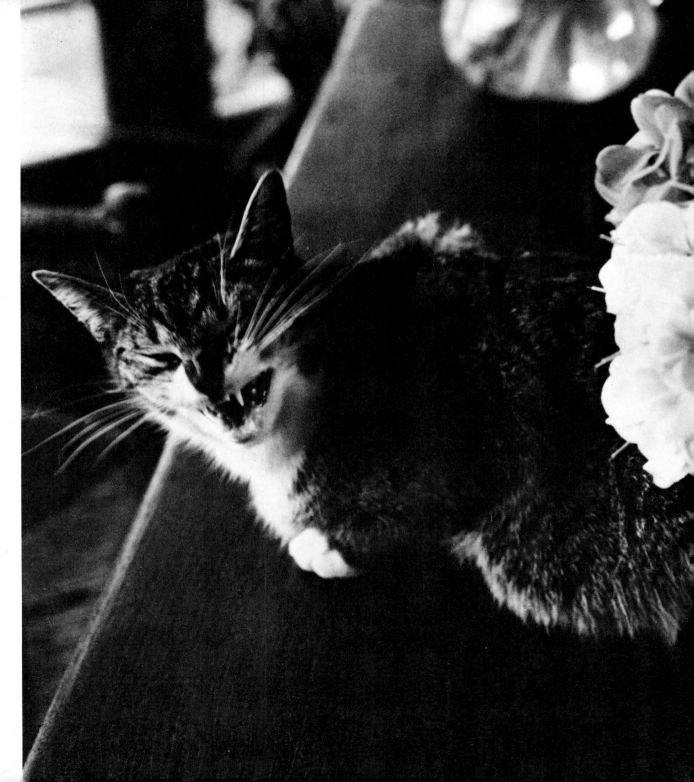

No life is so hard
that you can't
make it easier
by the way
you take it.

ELLEN GLASGOW

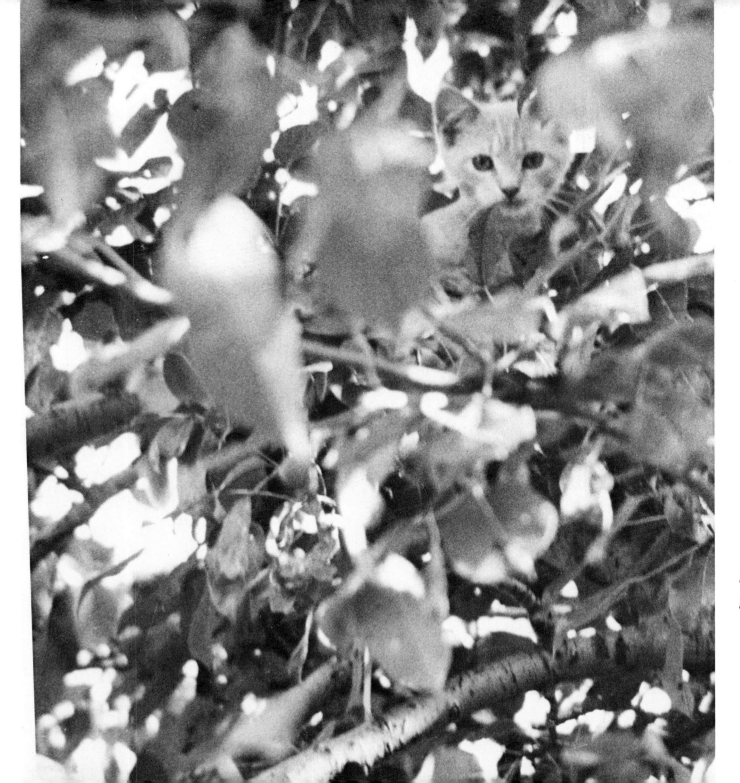

Heaven lies about us
in our infancy.

WILLIAM WORDSWORTH

Those move
easiest
who have
learned to dance.

ALEXANDER POPE

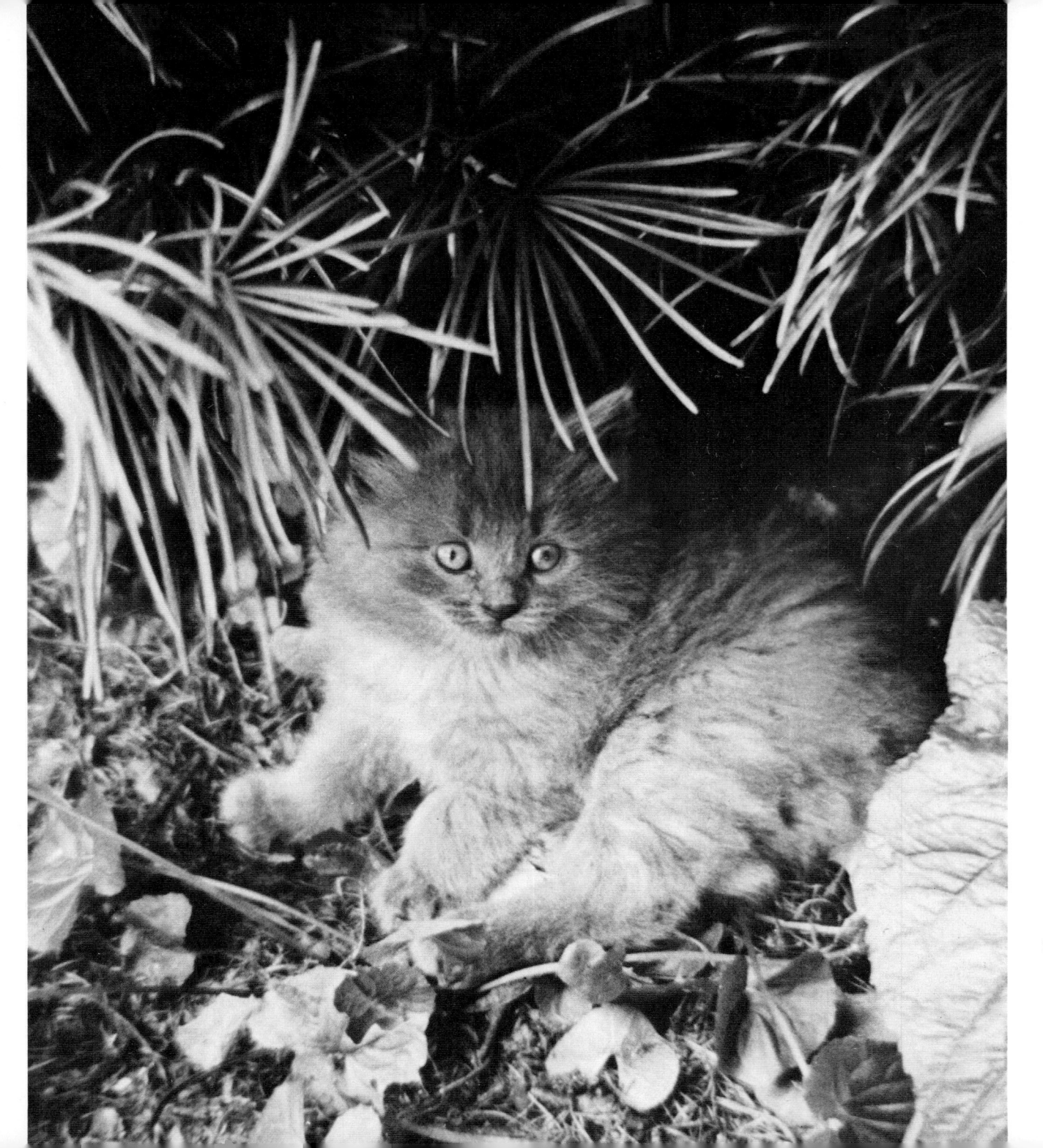

Young
in limbs,
in judgement
old.

WILLIAM SHAKESPEARE

*Idleness is the
root of all evil.*

GEORGE FARQUHAR

Thirst departs with drinking.

RABELAIS

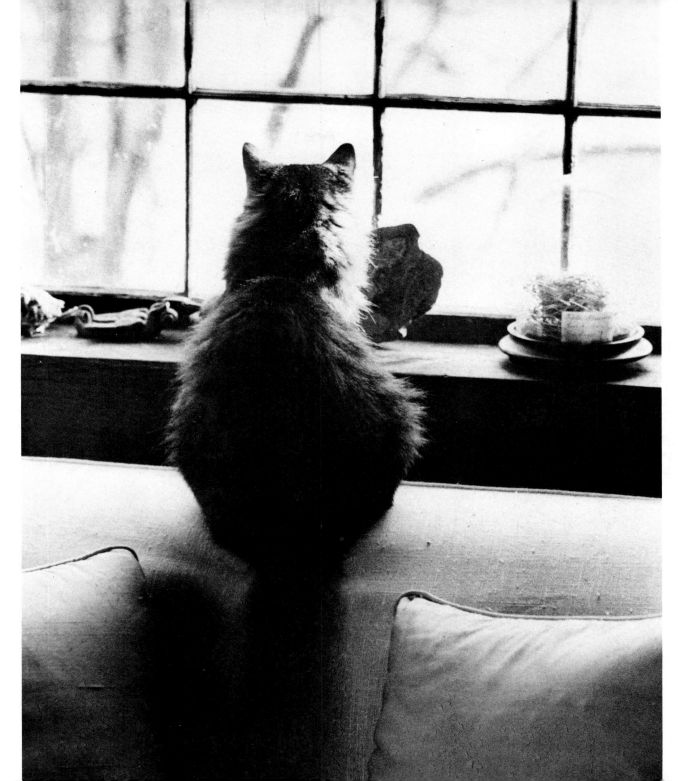

*Every hour of my
time is my own.*

PHILIP BARRY

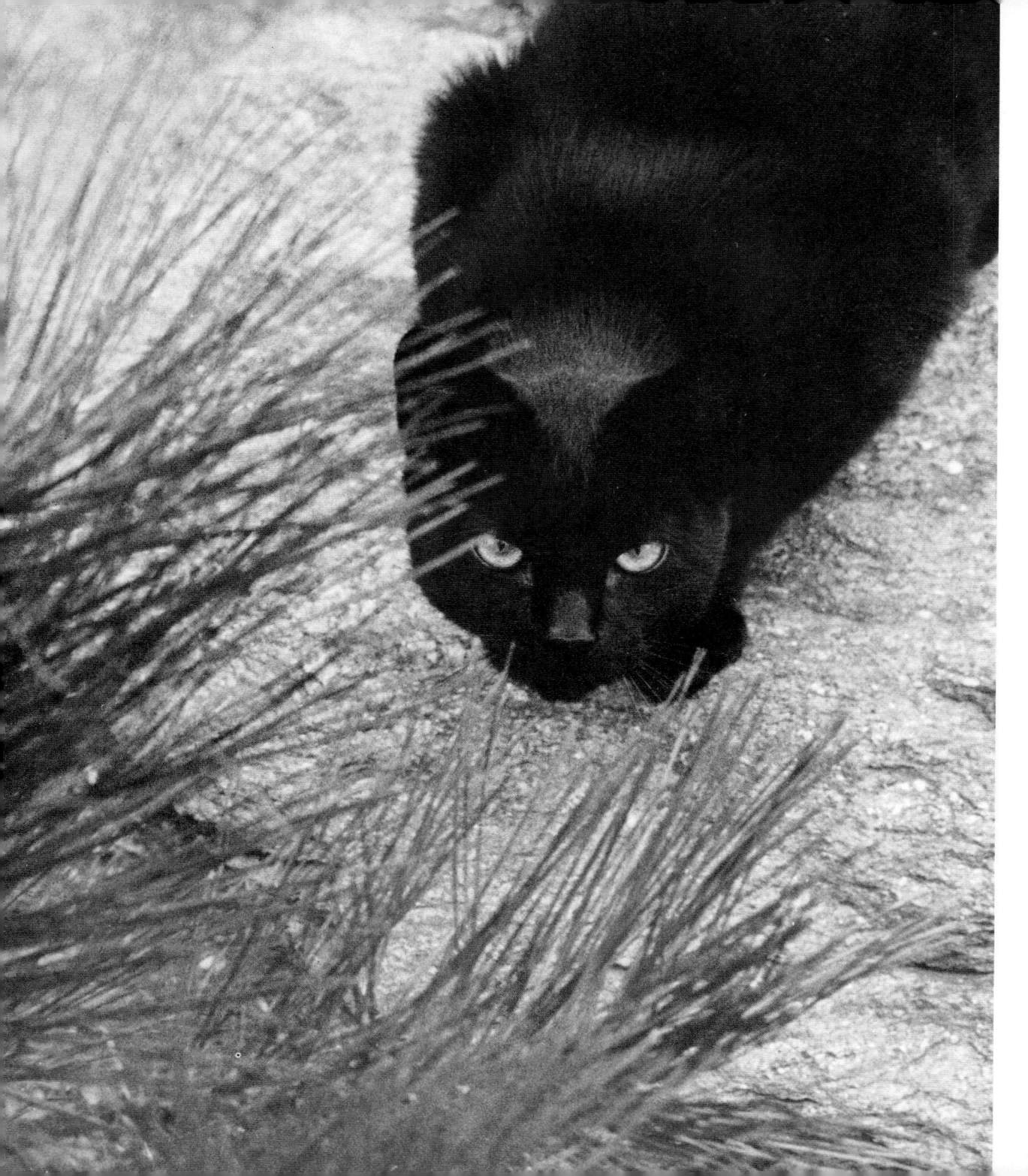

*He guides me
and the bird.*

ROBERT BROWNING

*One bad general
is better than
two good ones.*

NAPOLEON BONAPARTE

*The desire to
appear clever
often prevents
our being so.*

LA ROCHEFOUCAULD

All that I am,
or hope to be,
I owe to my
angel mother.

ABRAHAM LINCOLN

Where you are
is of no moment,
but only what
you are doing there.

PETRARCH

*It is often easier
to fight for
principles
than to live
up to them.*

ADLAI STEVENSON

I never think of the future. It comes soon enough.

ALBERT EINSTEIN

Walk and be happy,
walk and be healthy.

CHARLES DICKENS

An acute observer
can observe minutely
without being
observed.

JOHANN LAVATER

I have some knowledge of the world.

JOHN GALSWORTHY

*Poets are never
young . . . their
delicate ear hears
the far-off
whispers of
eternity.*

OLIVER WENDELL HOLMES

*The blood more stirs
to rouse a lion than
to start a hare.*

WILLIAM SHAKESPEARE

*Wisdom is
very wearisome.*

HÁFIZ

Alice

Ashley

Bird

Bootsie

Boy

Butterfly

Cotton

Daisy

Dandelion

Dorothy

Duff

Elizabeth

Faustus

Frisbee I

Frisbee II

Gertrude

Harold

Itty Bitty

| Lemon | Little Crazy | Little Lemon | Little Orange | Lola | Malevolence |

| Miss Gray | Mrs. Skeffington | Muff | Orlando | Ramona | Rascal |

| Sambo | Scout | Spats | Streak | Sylvia | Tiger Lily |

A Note About the Authors

Wilbur Pippin has been a professional photographer for many years. Ten years ago, he began photographing his cats in and around his Connecticut house for his own pleasure. At present there are fifteen cats in residence. Catwise is Mr. Pippin's first book, but his fashion photographs have appeared in most of America's leading magazines.

Marian Winters is a name well known to Broadway and television audiences. Miss Winters has won, among other awards, a Tony for her acting and an Emmy, as a playwright, for Animal Keepers, (included in a collection of her one-act plays, A Is for All, published by Dramatists Play Service). An avid reader, she was able to call on her memory for many of the quotes she used to caption these photos.

A Note About the Type

The text of this book was set in the film version of Optima, a typeface designed by Hermann Zapf from 1952-55 and issued in 1958. In designing Optima, Zapf created a truly new type form—a cross between the classic roman and a sans-serif face. So delicate are the stresses and balances in Optima that it rivals sans-serif faces in clarity and freshness and old-style faces in variety and interest.

This book was composed by Superior Printing, Champagne, Illinois. It was printed and bound by Halliday Lithographers, West Hanover, Massachusetts. Designed by Anne Pentola